We Move Together

Kelly Fritsch   Anne McGuire   Eduardo Trejos

We Move Together
© Kelly Fritsch, Anne McGuire, and Eduardo Trejos

E-ISBN: 9781849354059
Library of Congress Control Number: 2020946137

AK Press
370 Ryan Avenue #100
Chico, CA 95973
www.akpress.org
akpress@akpress.org

AK Press
33 Tower St.
Edinburgh EH6 7BN
Scotland
www.akuk.com
akuk@akpress.org

Please contact us to request the latest AK Press distribution catalog, which features books, pamphlets, zines, and stylish apparel published and/or distributed by AK Press. Alternatively, visit our websites for the complete catalog, latest news, and secure ordering

Cover lettering by Alana McCarthy—AlanaMcCarthy.com

Printed in Canada

All bodies are unique and essential. All bodies are whole.
All bodies have strengths and needs that must be met.
We are powerful not despite the complexities of our bodies,
but because of them. We move together, with no body
left behind. This is disability justice.

Aurora Levins Morales and Patty Berne

We
move fast.

Sometimes we have to wait.

Waiting can feel boring, frustrating, hard.
Waiting can also feel exciting...

...like butterflies,

like love.

We wait so we can
spend time together.

Like when all the fun and flavors of
ice cream are just one step out of reach.

We work together.

Kids and dogs.

Bodies and machines.

Bees and flowers.

Fish and water.

Relying on each other helps us get where we need to go.

Sometimes we find ourselves in unfamiliar places.

We wonder.

We get curious.

We might have more
questions than answers.

Our questions can help us learn to do things **differently.**

And discover new ways of **understanding each other.**

For the things that connect us
are also what **nourish us.**

Like roots and tubes
and straws and friends.

And these things that connect us are often what challenge us.

Sometimes we disagree about how to be together.

Solving one problem can create another and we don't always know how to make things better.

to take a break.

Even when we're by ourselves,
we never move alone.

Like feeling so close with someone
who's far. Like learning from others who
have come before. Their memories can

ground us,

soothe us,

move us.

You get proud
by practicing

Whether we're by ourselves, or surrounded by many, our small movements can turn into big movements.

We move together.

Ideas and Illustrations: A Closer Look

How We Move

When we move together, **everyone moves differently!**

Some people move on **bikes** or **push scooters**. Other people use **crutches**, **canes**, or **walkers**.

People also move using **wheelchairs**— which can be electrically powered or physically propelled—or **mobility scooters**. Some people have a **ventilator** attached to their wheelchair which is a machine with a tube that helps them to breathe.

These tools are called **assistive devices** because they make it easier for people to get around, to find their balance, or take a rest.

We also move using **buses**, **strollers**, **dogs**, and even **shopping carts**!

Ableism

Because everyone moves differently, it can be hard to find places where we can all be together. Some places weren't designed to welcome everyone and that means that sometimes, some of us get **left out**. This is ableism.

Ableism is a form of discrimination. It wrongly considers only some bodies, minds, and behaviors to be normal, worthy, and valuable.

Ableism assumes that being able to run fast on two legs is better than zooming around in a wheelchair, using crutches, or moving slowly. Ableism assumes that a body that can sit still or quietly in a desk at school is better than a body that needs to squirm, wiggle, stim, and move around.

The idea that some bodies, minds, and ways of moving are better than others often excludes disabled people and can lead to hurtful **labels**, like when people get called dumb, ugly, stupid, crazy, or lame.

Ableism creates **barriers** for disabled people, making it hard to meet friends, learn at school, find a place to live, get a job, participate in community events, or even go for ice cream!

Disability justice activists like **Patty Berne**, **Leroy Moore**, **Eli Clare**, and **Mia Mingus** remind us that ableism is connected to other forms of injustice like racism and gender inequality. Disabled people are valuable members of all our communities: we must all work together to fight ableism and build a more just world for everyone.

Accessibility

Wheelchair-user **Luke Anderson** noticed that he was being prevented from going into many of the stores, restaurants, and other buildings in his neighborhood because they had at least one stair to get in and out. Luke worked together with other people in his community to start the **StopGap Community Ramp** project.

Through StopGap, disabled and non-disabled people come together to build portable wooden ramps that make our community spaces more welcoming and useable for more people. So far, this project has made over 2000 brightly coloured ramps worldwide! The StopGap ramp project is an example of **accessibility**—one way of making sure all people can enter, move around in, and use the spaces we share.

Another example of accessibility is **curb cuts**. These mini ramps built into the sidewalk make it easier for people using wheelchairs and

walkers, or people pushing strollers and delivery carts to get from the sidewalk to the road. Sometimes curb cuts have bumps on them—this is called **tactile pavement** and it alerts blind or visually impaired people moving with **white-canes** or **guide dogs** that they are about to leave the sidewalk and move onto the street.

Accessibility is more than just physical changes to our buildings or environments. Making things accessible can also mean removing financial barriers, using unscented products, learning new ways of communicating, and making sure friends feel welcome and are included. Access is something we can practice and build everyday. Activists at the **Disability Visibility Project** say that **"Access is Love"**—that making something accessible is a loving way of making sure we all belong.

Disability Arts & Culture

Disability art pushes us to think about disability in new ways and imagine new possibilities for moving together.

Carmen Papalia is blind and a non-visual artist who uses a long white cane to help him move around. He created an art project where he uses his white cane to lead sighted people on walks with their eyes closed. When people follow Papalia and his cane, they learn unique non-visual ways of moving together.

Carmen is not the only disabled artist. There are so many that there is even an entire art gallery named **Tangled** in Toronto, Canada for disabled artists and their work! Some disabled artists **dance** using their wheelchairs, or **paint**, or write **poetry**. Others create **sculptures**. At Tangled, visitors can interact with the art using different senses. Sometimes you can even **touch** the art!

How We Communicate

Moving together means learning about the many ways we communicate.

Sometimes communication is about using **words** and **voices**.

Sometimes communication means using **non-verbal gestures**, **body language**, and **facial expressions**. For example, people might communicate with their eyes, a wide smile, slouched shoulders, by flapping their hands, or raising a hand in the air.

Sometimes communication can look like someone yelling, or crying, or putting their hands over their ears.

Or, sometimes people communicate by simply moving their body away from the group.

Deaf people and others who have trouble hearing spoken words often talk using **sign language**.

Non-speaking people may choose to use pictures, tablets, or computers to communicate.

People also say what they need to say using **placards**, **art**, or **music**... or even **clothing**!

In 2017, disability activist Annie Segarra put the words "**The Future is Accessible**" on a t-shirt to encourage people to think about disability and accessibility in their communities and everyday lives.

There is no one best way to communicate and there are lots of people, books, and websites that can help us learn a new language. When we discover new ways of communicating, we can experience our world differently. Some Deaf people refer to their communication differences as **Deaf Gain** (rather than hearing loss) to celebrate how Deaf ways of thinking and communicating open up meaningful ways of being together.

Moving Together Isn't Always Easy...

It isn't always easy to move together because sometimes we have different ideas and needs.

For example, plastic pollution is a big problem for our environment. Plastic water bottles, bags, and straws are being dumped into our oceans and seas; they are polluting our waterways and harming many different species like turtles and fish.

One solution people have come up with is to **ban plastic straws** from being used in restaurants or stores.

Banning straws solves one problem but creates another. While all of us depend on clean oceans and ecosystems, some people also depend on plastic tubes and straws to help them drink or eat liquid foods. For these people, plastic **tubes and straws are access**: it is what helps them live!

The slogan "**Nothing about us without us!**" is a reminder that disabled people have often been left out of conversations about issues that are important to our lives.

Disability activist **Alice Wong** says that our movements are stronger when we work together. Disability movements are deeply connected to other social justice movements. We need to listen and learn from each other's experiences and perspectives so we can come up with new and creative ideas for how to solve the problems we all face.

Disability Community

It can be hard to live in our world when your body or mind is not considered best. This led disabled writer **Laura Hershey** to write the poem **You Get Proud by Practicing**.

Reading words and hearing stories by disabled people —both past and present— can connect us to rich **disability histories**, **cultures**, **communities**, and **social movements**.

Finding a community of people with whom we can share experiences and ideas can help us understand our own bodies and minds in new and powerful ways.

We're in this together: moving together with other disabled people and our allies, we can imagine and work towards building a better world and future.

Kelly Fritsch is a disabled writer, educator, and parent living in Ottawa with her mischievous cat, Loulou. She is an assistant professor in the Department of Sociology and Anthropology at Carleton University and co-editor of KEYWORDS FOR RADICALS: THE CONTESTED VOCABULARY OF LATE-CAPITALIST STRUGGLE (2015, AK Press).

Anne McGuire is an associate professor in the program for Critical Studies in Equity and Solidarity at the University of Toronto, where she teaches courses in disability studies and disabled childhoods. She is the author of WAR ON AUTISM: ON THE CULTURAL LOGIC OF NORMATIVE VIOLENCE (2016, University of Michigan Press).

Eduardo Trejos is a Costa Rican multi-disciplinary artist. A lover of color, insatiable reader, and parent of two boys, he currently lives in Toronto where he works as a graphic designer.